Ramming the Shears

Back cover photograph by courtesy of
The National Gallery of Victoria.

Photograph: Wayne Ludbey

This book is copyright. Apart from any fair dealing for
the purposes of private study, research, criticism or review,
as permitted under the Copyright Act, no part may be
reproduced by any process without written permission.
All inquiries should be addressed to the publisher.

Copyright © Michael Leunig 1985

First published by Dynamo Press 1985

Dynamo Press,
Dynamo House P/L,
38a Murphy Street,
Richmond 3121,
Victoria, Australia.

National Library of Australia
Cataloguing-in-publication data.

Leunig, Michael,
   Ramming the Shears.

ISBN 0 949266 13 2

1. Caricatures and cartoons — Australia.
2. Australian wit and humor. Pictorial. I. Title.

7415994

Printed in Australia by Globe Press Pty. Ltd.

Ramming the Shears

A COLLECTION OF DRAWINGS

BY

Michael Leunig

DYNAMO PRESS

MELBOURNE

The state of things.

Spring

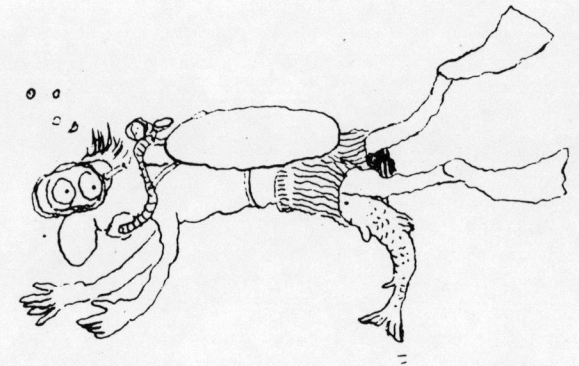

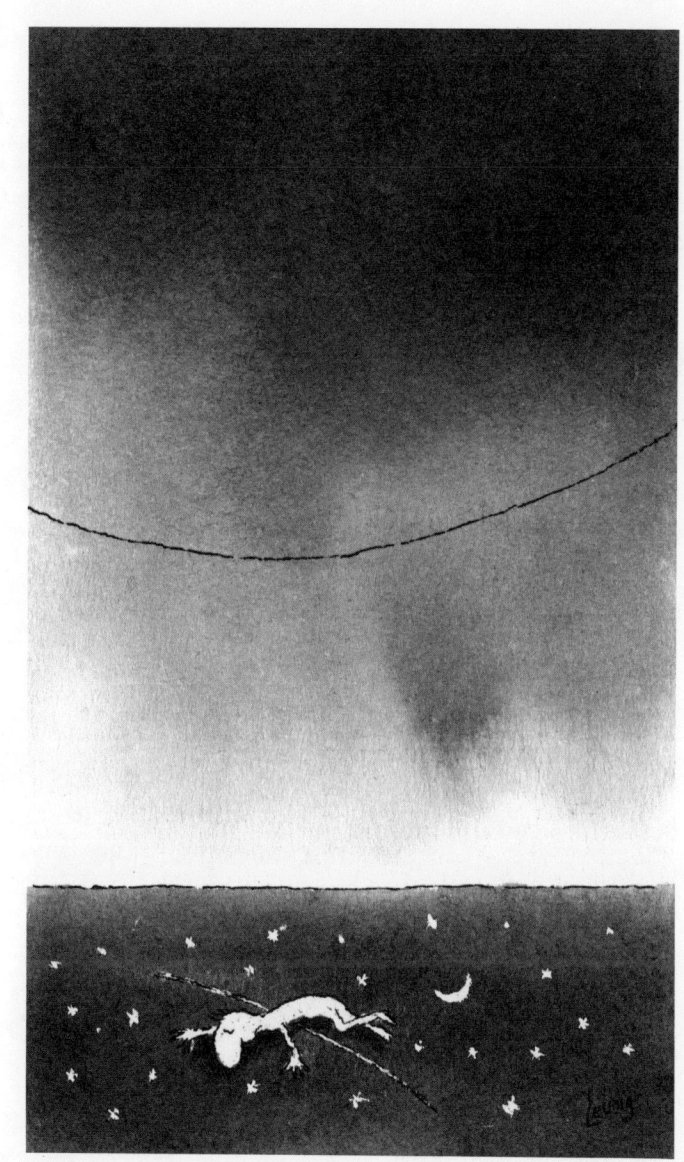

There was once a man who became so knowing and sceptical that he could see through everything.

While talking to friends he would look through their heads at paintings on the wall behind them.

He even saw through the paintings and the walls they hung on: he knew all about art and architecture.

He was so travelled that the horizon too lost its mystery: he knew what was beyond it

His vision circumnavigated the earth unimpeded until he was looking at the back of his own head....

......which was so transparent to him that his vision penetrated it and came out through his eyes again.

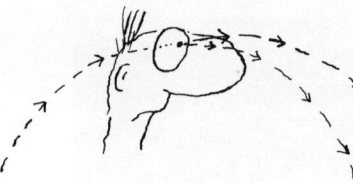

He was now seeing nothing twice.... three times.... hundreds of times a minute as his vision looped the earth at the speed of light.

THIS CAUSES THE EYES TO TAKE ON AN UNFOCUSED, SAD AND LONELY LOOK WHICH MAY APPEAR ROMANTIC.
IT IS <u>NOT</u> ROMANTIC.

IT IS NEW ROMANTIC.

leunig

What are you looking for...?	I'm looking for the cutting edge.
THE WHAT?	You know... the cutting edge..
it cuts through things...	it cuts through all the rubbish.
...it cuts through the years.... and the heart...	it cuts through all we know and understand...
IT CUTS THROUGH THE WAY THINGS ARE..... it just goes....	..SLASH
...and suddenly everything is different and thrilling..	IT'S THE WONDERFUL CUTTING EDGE. have you seen it....?
NO...	Did you look in the cupboard under the sink...?

Leunig

EASE YOUR WAY TO PUBLIC WEEPING

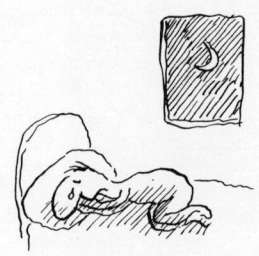
Begin alone... quietly.... at night... A few little sobs on the pillow.

Then weep in the afternoon... on the verandah.

Now for the mirror. Look in the mirror and weep for yourself.

Weep for other living things.... NOW YOU HAVE MASTERED BASIC WEEPING.

ADVANCED WEEPING

Weep with another person in a dark paddock...

WEEP IN A BUSTLING CROWD.

WEEP ON STAGE IN CONCERT.... CLASSICAL PUBLIC WEEPING etc.   Leunig

There will come a time when sanity will all be done by computers.

Home births will be normal but homes will become more temporary.

There will be supermarkets devoted entirely to the sale of hair conditioners and shampoos.

Full flush, half flush, quarter flush toilets. Simple, natural functions will increasingly involve decision making.

Time will speed up. Humans will live a greater number of years but their lives will actually be shorter.

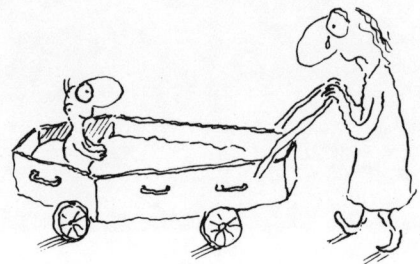

Whatever happens, a child born tomorrow will be the same as a child born two thousand years ago.

Leunig

"I just feel so incredibly free."

CALENDAR OF WEEKLY EVENTS

Mr. Curly sees the "Great Impressionists" at the National Gallery.

"David . . . you have captured my elusive, non-conformist soul and you are truly a genius."

"Hey look, wow! Hey fabuloso! Under these pine boards. Genuine fifties Laminex with silver flecks. WOOOOWEE!!"

The best way to paint.

"Good evening constable. I was just enjoying a spot of the old rap dancing!"

Bitter Disappointment.

Ahh summer....!
Le Specs....
Le Tan......

Le Flies
Le Broken Glass.

Le Bushfire!

Le Fight in Le Pub

Le Car Accident.

Le Depression
Le Madness
Le Hot North Wind.

LE SUMMER!

WHAT AIDS WILL DO TO YOUR SEX LIFE

AIDS MEANS THE END OF CASUAL SEX. SAY GOODBYE TO THONGS AND T-SHIRT SEX...

JOKING, FRIENDLY "HAVE A CUP OF TEA" SEX. EXPERIMENTAL JAZZY, CUBIST SEX

FREE FORM, OUTDOOR PEOPLE'S STREET SEX. DROUGHTY, RURAL MAKE-DO TIN SHED SEX. SAY GOODBYE TO ALL THAT.

SAY HELLO TO FORMAL SEX. CLASSICAL, HIGHBROW, SERIOUS MONOGAMOUS SEX.

DILIGENT, EXTERNALLY EXAMINED AND ASSESSED THEORY AND PRAC. WITH HONORS SEX

RESPONSIBLE, SENSIBLE PHOTO-REALIST SEX. STRICTLY STRUCTURED "BEGINNING, MIDDLE AND END" SEX ETC. ETC. ETC. SAY HELLO TO ALL THAT.

Leunig.

TIME TO GET YOUR TOMATOES IN

Tending your tomato plants is one of life's great simple pleasures but there are pitfalls

Nuclear winter, caused by global nuclear war can delay ripening.

Tomato stakes are best hammered in under the cover of darkness to avoid being spotted by B.L.F. officials.

On the brighter side: the chances of catching genital herpes or AIDS from the handling of tomatoes are fairly low.

Bikie wars and shoot-outs in the garden during flowering can seriously affect cropping.

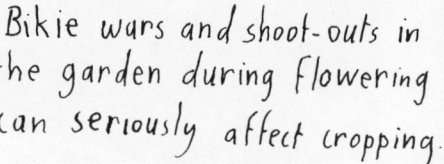

Certainly... tomato tending has its worries but it's all worthwhile when you stand in the garden on a warm summers day and sink your fangs into a firm, ripe freshly picked tomato.

Awful aspects of spring. The new dog digs up the old dog.

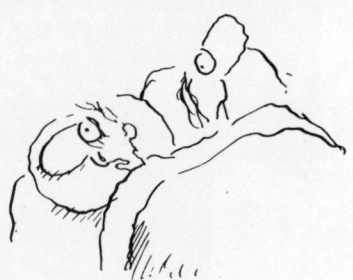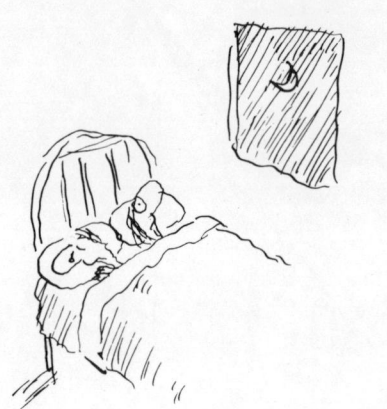

"Some enchanted evening . . . you may see a stranger.
You may see a stranger . . . across a crowded room."

Isn't it a funny name for a dance . . . the "Foxtrot".

A SPRING MYSTERY.

WHY DO BIRDS DO THIS ...... WHEN THEY COULD DO THIS.

NESTS FOR RENT

Leunig

A Winter's Poem

A clever creature is the snake
Who spends his winter not awake
He snuggles in his long thin bed
And brews up venom in his head.

The human is a different sort
He spends the winter watching sport.
He yells abuse in concrete stands
And empties out his poison glands.

Winter.

THINGS TO DO IN AUTUMN

Watch the same old faces getting the same old awards.

Bash the same old head against the same old wall.

Wear the same old heart on the same old sleeve.

Put the same old foot in the same old foothold

Watch the autumn leaves falling.

Salute them for having the decency to fall when it was time

The Autumn Festival of Lust and Passion.

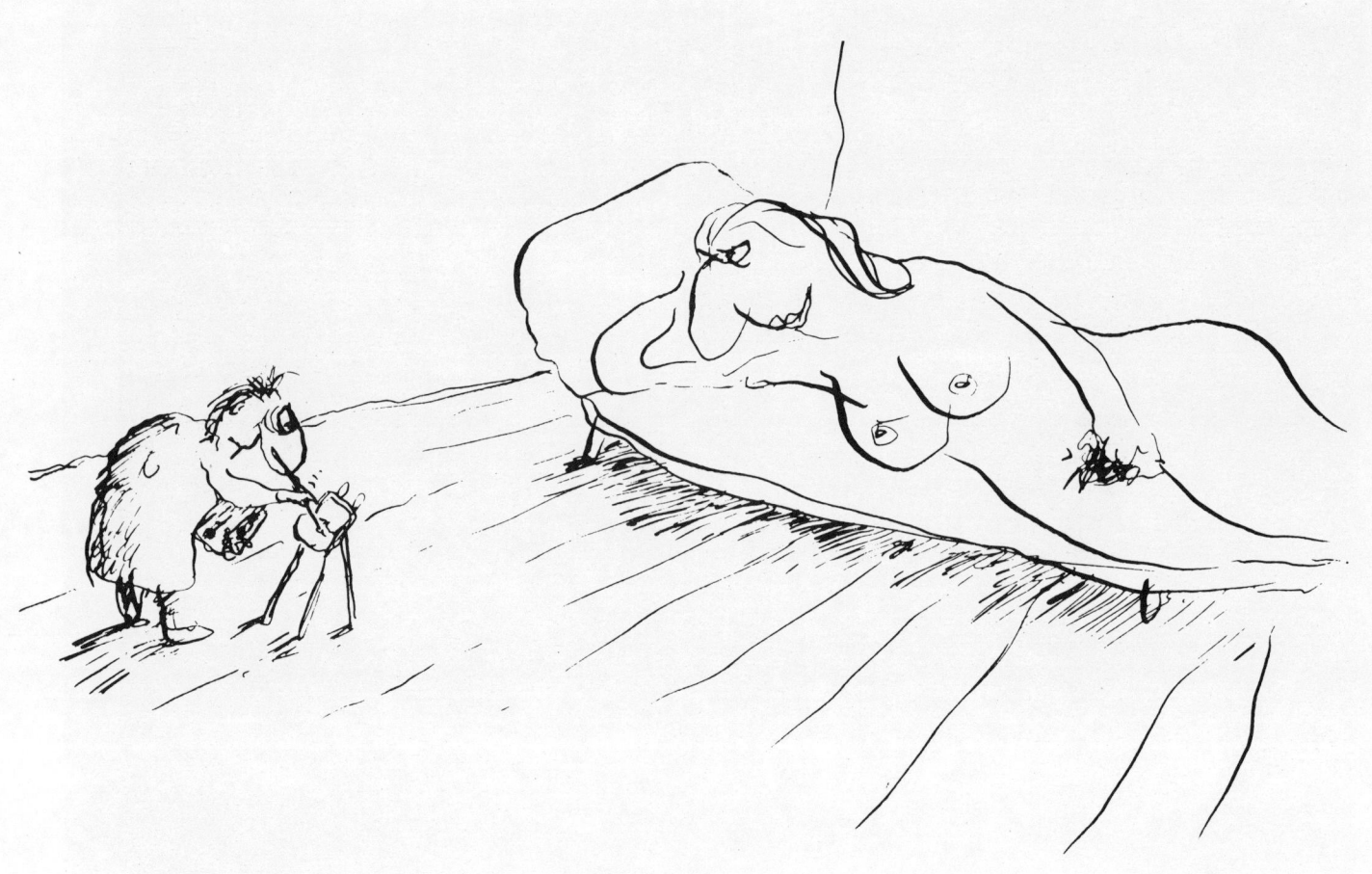

"Come home to the garden with me Mary, to the roses and the old plum tree. We'll put the chain on the gate and make a lovely cup of tea."

People crawl along streets. Lamp posts droop.

Bus shelters wilt.

Statues hang limply from pedestals.

Spoons droop from cups. Teapot spouts flop on dirty old table cloths.

Conductors batons and violins sag.

GLOOM AND DOOM....... everywhere things are declining.

The Affair.

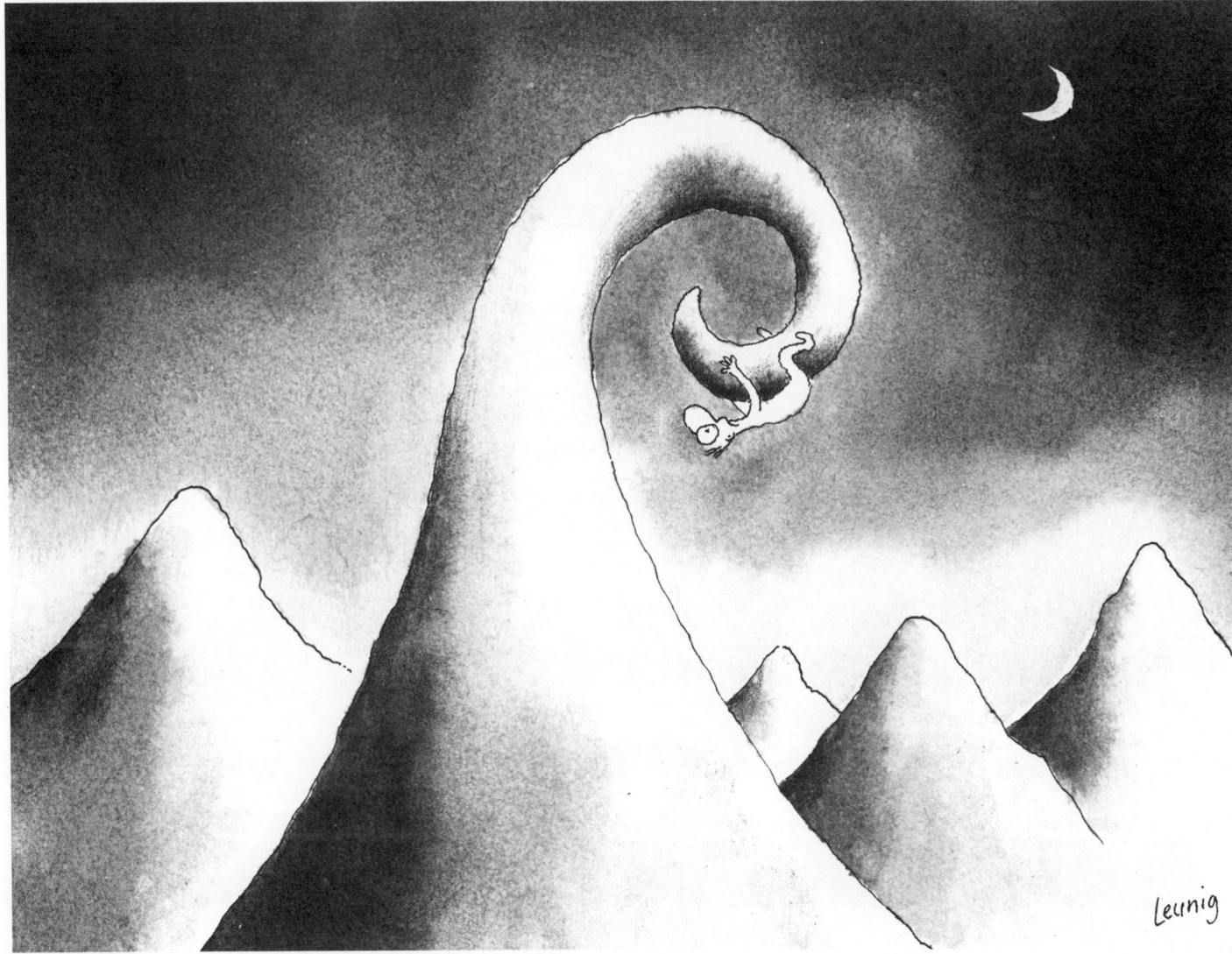

The Cruel Sea.

The Garden Gate.